May the animals come to life
under the magical touch of your pencil,
and may the joy of creating and exploring the world spread through each
drawing."

Claude Alvarez
2024

ARTIST PROPERTY:

let's see its colors?

Aa

Alligator

Aa

Anteater

Bb

Bear

Bb

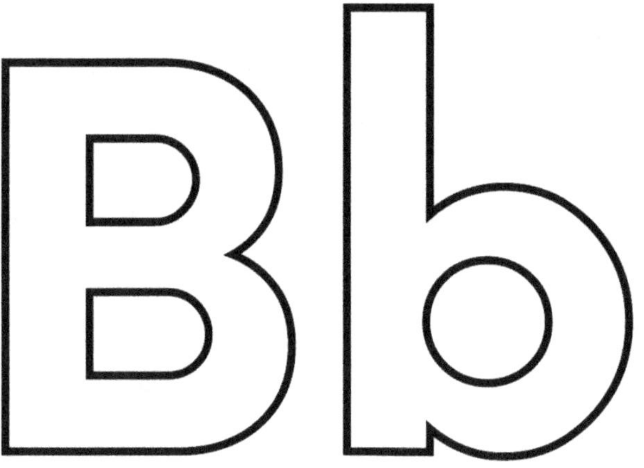

Butterfly

C c

Chameleon

Cc

Cheetah

Dd

Dolphin

Dd

Duck

E e

Elephant

Ff

Flamingo

Ff

Fox

Gg

Giraffe

Hh

Hippopotamus

Ii

Iguana

Jj

Jaguar

Kk

Kangaroo

Ll

Lion

Mm

Macaw

Mm

Manatee

Nn

Narwhal

Ostrich

P p

Penguin

Qq

Quokka

R r

Rabbit

R r

Raccon

Ss

Sloth

Tt

Tiger

Tt

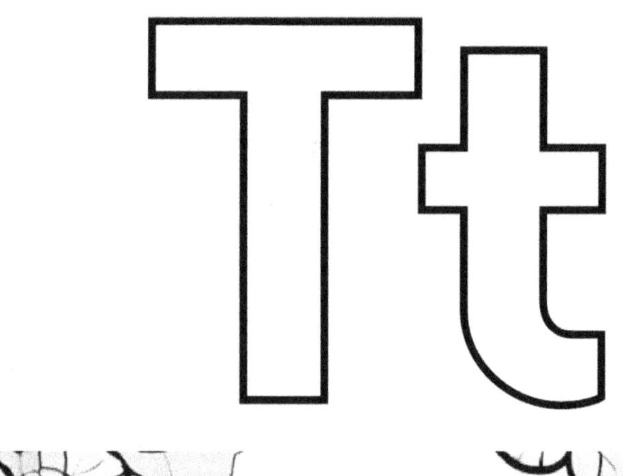

Turtle

U u

Uakari

V v

Vulture

Ww

Walrus

Ww

Wolf

Xenops

Yy

Yosemite Toad

Zz

Zebra